PRAISE FOR NOAH ST. JOHN

"To say that Noah St. John changed our lives is the understatement of the century. Before hiring Noah as my personal coach, I had a brochure website that wasn't bringing in any money. Today, I have my own online store that makes me money in my sleep. Thank you, Noah, for bringing out the greatness in me that I didn't even know I had!"

—Dr. Stacey Cooper, Chiropractor

"Before I heard Noah speak, I had been a failure at everything I touched. After using his methods, I built the largest infill development company in Nashville with over $40 million in sales. Thank you, Noah; keep doing what you're doing because a lot of people need you!"

—Britnie Turner Keane, Aerial Development Group

"I highly recommend Dr. Noah St. John as a keynote speaker because he's not only different from other speakers, he also truly cares about his clients and resonates on a deep emotional level with his audience. He's dynamic, impactful, inspiring, motivating, and professional—in short, the PERFECT speaker!"

—Lauren Ashley Kay, Meeting Planner

"Dr. Noah St. John has been a Legend in the industry of speaking and motivating for many years. His reputation as a home run speaker, powerful coach, and performance expert is among the best in the world. More importantly, his home life, family, and ability to balance both business and the living of a wonderful life are inspiring to his peers and clients. He is an example to all who know him."

—Jason Hewlett, CSP, CFAE, The Promise to the One

"Noah's methods helped me get through a particularly challenging time in my life. If you're thinking about hiring Noah as a coach, trainer, or speaker, don't think about it another minute—just DO it, because his strategies have the power to change lives!"

—Mari Smith, Facebook Marketing Expert

"Noah's methods can transform your life and help you create the masterpiece you truly want and are capable of achieving."

—John Assaraf, The Secret

"Noah's training was instrumental in helping me bounce back and into major profits. His insights on removing head trash are unlike anything I've ever seen!"

—Ray Higdon, Time Money Freedom

"Noah St. John helped me gain the mental edge I was looking for. His methods helped me perform at my highest level without strain, and I saw better results immediately using his system."

—Andre Branch, NFL Football Player

"Before being coached by Noah, I was holding myself back out of fear. Since working with Noah, I've built a multi-million dollar company in less than two years. I highly recommend coaching with Noah, because I guarantee it will change your life, like it changed mine!"

—Tim Taylor, Real Estate Professional

"Noah St. John has been at the forefront of the business coaching industry for more than two decades now. He's the best in the business when it comes to helping entrepreneurs skyrocket their results in record time. If you want to take your business to a whole new level without the stress or overwhelm, hire Noah St. John TODAY. You'll be glad you did!"

—Anik Singal, Lurn.com 8-Figure CEO

"Noah has created something magical. I've been studying personal growth for more than 25 years and his insights take it to the next level!"

—Jenny McCarthy, Judge on The Masked Singer

"I've known Noah for a long time and he was someone who early on gravitated to my message of bringing massive value to his audience."

—Gary Vaynerchuk, CEO of VaynerMedia

"Noah St. John's work is about discovering within ourselves what we should have known all along — we are truly powerful beings with unlimited potential."

—Stephen Covey, The 7 Habits of Highly Effective People

ALSO BY NOAH ST. JOHN, PhD

The 7-Figure Life: How to Leverage The 4 Focus Factors
for More Wealth and Happiness

Power Habits®: The New Science for
Making Success Automatic®

AFFORMATIONS®: The Miracle of Positive Self-Talk

Millionaire AFFORMATIONS®:
The Magic Formula That Will Make You Rich

Millionaire AFFORMATIONS® Journal: The Magic
Habit Formula That Will Make You Rich

Take Out Your Head Trash About Money

The Secret Code of Success

Permission to Succeed®

Available at NoahStJohn.com
or wherever books are sold

The 7-Figure Expert

Your Ultimate Guide to a Life of More Impact,
Influence and Financial Freedom

Dr. Noah St. John

Success Clinic International, LLC

Published 2023 by Success Clinic International, LLC
SuccessClinic.com
First edition: 2023

Library of Congress Cataloging-in-Publication Data is available upon
request

ISBN: 9798393933098

10 9 8 7 6 5 4 3 2 1

*This book is dedicated to #Afformers and
#AfformationWarriors around the world:
Those brave souls who ask better questions
to make this a better world
for all of God's creatures.*

*And to my beautiful wife, Babette,
for being the best example of a Loving Mirror
I've ever met.*

Contents

CHAPTER 1
Introducing My 7-Figure Expert Formula

"The secret to happiness is freedom.
And the secret to freedom is courage."
—*Thucydides*

My big goal for this book is to show you how you can instantly shatter your limiting beliefs that are putting a ceiling on your income, using one simple process that can take place in as little as five minutes a day, using my legendary 7-Figure Expert Formula.

I'd like to point out that as fantastic as it is to turn your annual income into your monthly income (or even your weekly income), I feel what is even more important is **winning your life back.**

Because what good is having lots of money if you don't have a LIFE?

For example, a lot of the so-called "gurus" out there teach "hustle and grind," right? They say that all you need to do to make more money is "work 18 hours a day and don't take any breaks and never see your family. Sound good?" No, that sucks!

That's not what I want for my life, and I'll bet it's not

what you want, either. The fact is, your business should exist to serve your life, not the other way around.

So the point is, it's not only about the money, it's about **winning your life back.**

How I Know My Formula Works

Because I've turned my annual income into my daily income simply by following my own 7-Figure Expert Formula that I'm going to teach you in this book. Which means, whether you want to turn your annual income into your monthly income, your weekly income, or even your daily income, it's not only possible, but I've proven it over 3,000 times with myself and my clients.

YOUR BUSINESS SHOULD EXIST TO SERVE YOUR LIFE, NOT THE OTHER WAY AROUND.

You've heard the famous quote by Charles Dickens: *"It was the best of times, it was the worst of times."* Well, over the last several years, as we all know, for millions of people around the world, it's been the worst of times. Because of the pandemic, millions of people lost their jobs, their livelihoods, their businesses, and lost loved ones. For them, these past few years have indeed been "the worst of times."

However, for my company, SuccessClinic.com, as well as for my clients, these last few years have been "the best of times."

For example, I was able to purchase a gorgeous new

home that our clients call Success Manor, a 6000-square-foot mansion on a hill. So for my company and my clients, these last few years have been the best of times.

Is This Opportunity For You?

What does all this mean for you? It means that if my formula works for me and my clients, it can work for you, too! You simply have to put it in place, using the 5-step formula I'm going to give you in this book.

So the question is, **Is this opportunity for you?** This opportunity is for you if...

1. You're tired of the 9-5 and want to escape the rat race.

2. You have a business and are looking for new income streams.

   IF THIS SOUNDS LIKE YOU, THIS OPPORTUNITY IS FOR YOU.

3. You're looking for a side business that you can do part time.

4. You're a stay-at-home parent or retiree looking for some extra income.

5. You're seeking the online freedom lifestyle.

The Big Change Happening Right Now

According to Google Trends, interest in mental health solutions is at an all time high. Have you noticed that more people are talking about mental health now than ever before?

Even as recently as 2011, very few people were talking about mental health. It was, in fact, a taboo subject. Then over the last few years, interest in mental health has gone WAY up and a big part of that is the pandemic we've just come out of.

What's fascinating is that I've been teaching mental health solutions for experts and entrepreneurs for more than 25 years! Which means that finally, the world is beginning to catch on to the power and importance of what I've been teaching my clients for more than a quarter century.

The Big Risk You're Facing Right Now

The big problem you're facing right now is that running your own business isn't just a physically demanding job. It's a mentally and emotionally demanding one as well. Wouldn't you agree?

It's interesting that the "hustle and grinders" tell you to just keep hustling and grinding, and forget about your mental health—to say nothing of your physical and emotional health.

Which means that in addition to the big change in the world and the big problem you're facing, you're also facing a big risk: *without the proper systems in place, you, your business and your very livelihood are at risk.*

In other words, if you don't put the right systems in place, for your mental and emotional health, and also for making more money in less time, your business and your very livelihood are at risk right now.

THIS IS THE BIGGEST RISK YOU'RE FACING RIGHT NOW.

The good news is, you don't have to risk that anymore! Because when you follow my 7-Figure Expert Formula, you can remove the risk and stop paying the price of sacrificing your time for money, which means you can start making a lot more money while winning your life back.

Who I Am and Why You Should Listen to Me

I grew up poor in a rich neighborhood.

I know that's a total cliché, but it's totally true. I grew up in a little town called Kennebunkport, Maine, which is one of the wealthiest communities in New England, but my family was dirt poor. I mean that literally, because we lived at the bottom of a dirt road in a drafty, unfinished house that my parents ended up losing a foreclosure when I was just 15 years old.

From a very young age, I was painfully exposed to the

gap between the Haves and the Have-Nots. The Haves was everyone else in the community, and the Have-Nots was my family.

You know those "motivational" speakers who get onstage and say things like, "We were poor, but we were happy because we didn't know we were poor?"

Well, in my family, we freakin' knew we were poor! Because my mother (bless her heart) reminded us every day that we were poor and miserable. So no, it wasn't happy—it sucked!

In fact, I hated that life of poverty and fear and lack and not-enoughness. That's what I grew up with in my family, yet I saw that right down the street there was great wealth and abundance. So from the time I was very little, I said to myself, *"How the heck do I get from here to there?"*

Of course, there was no one there to help me, so I did the only thing that I could think to do—I went to the library and started reading all these books on personal growth and success. I devoured the classics of self-help: Dale Carnegie, Napoleon Hill, Stephen Covey and more. And I really, really tried to put them to work.

I worked really hard, but I never could get them to work. At the age of 25, because I was so frustrated, depressed, and lonely, I decided to commit suicide. At the very last minute, my life was spared. But I didn't know why.

So I went on another long journey to answer the question: *"What is my purpose here on Earth?"* I went back to the library and started reading the classics of spiritual growth: Ernest Holmes, Louise Hay, Marianne Williamson, Neale Donald Walsch, Deepak Chopra, and the like.

Finding My Life's Purpose

Then in 1997, I had two epiphanies that changed my life. My first epiphany was in April 1997, when I discovered my now-legendary **AFFORMATIONS® Method** to instantly change your subconscious beliefs.

My second epiphany occurred in October 1997, when I discovered the condition I called *success anorexia* that explains why so many smart, creative, talented people hold themselves back from the level of success they're capable of.

Incredibly, both of those discoveries were landmarks in the history of the personal development industry, because they represented breaks with traditional success literature that had let so many people down—people like me.

As a result, I decided to launch my company, which I named **SuccessClinic. com**, in a 300-square-foot basement apartment with

THESE TWO DISCOVERIES FORMED MY LIFE'S PURPOSE.

$800 to my name and a book on HTML. When I launched my company, I had nothing: I didn't know anything about marketing, sales, bookkeeping or how to run a successful business.

Remember being online in the '90s? It was like trying

to build a house with a rock and some sticks! There was no social media, no Facebook, no YouTube. In fact, my company is seven months older than Google!

Getting Screwed By The Gurus

In fact, I had nothing but a dream. A dream to help people and to make a difference in the world—and Steve Jobs put it, "To put a dent in the universe."

Because I didn't know anything about how to run a successful business, as money would come in, I would simply invest it back in myself and my own education. Unfortunately, I ended up giving a lot of money to a lot of gurus who can't teach their way out of a paper bag!

As a result, 10 years later in January 2007, I ended up $40,000 in credit card debt, and I had to move into my parents' basement. Which means I went from basement number one in 1997 with $800 to my name, to basement number two ten years later with $40,000 in debt. Try that on for size!

EVERYTHING YOU DESIRE IS ON THE OTHER SIDE OF FEAR.

As you can imagine, I was very frustrated, angry, and confused. Of course, my parents told me over and over again that I should quit and find something else to do with my life. From their perspective, it had been 10 years and I had nothing to show for it, except being $40,000 in debt. So they told me that I should get a job and forget this whole entrepreneurial thing.

Have you ever been in a position like that? Where you've been working hard for a long time with little to show for it, and you're not sure if you should quit or keep going.

Maybe the people close to you are saying that you should quit and give up. Not because they don't believe in you, but because they don't want to see you in pain.

For me, I knew that I couldn't give up, I knew that I had a mission, a message that was very important—not just to me, but to the world. A message that people needed to hear. There was just one problem: even after all that money I'd spent, I couldn't find someone who could actually help me get my message out and make money doing it.

The One Decision That Changed Everything

That's when I made the one decision that changed my whole life, because I realized two very important things. One, that if you keep doing the same thing, you'll keep getting the same results. Two, that **everything you desire is on the other side of fear.**

That's when I made the one decision that changed everything, which was I decided to finally hire my first real business coach. Rather than going to all those gurus who can't teach their way out of a paper bag, I hired my first real business coach—someone who had a SYSTEM for making money online, and more importantly, someone who could TEACH me that system.

That's when everything changed for me—I got invited to speak across the country and around the world; I became a #1 best-selling author for the first time; I appeared on TV, radio and podcasts in front of millions of people; and best of all, I moved to Ohio and met this gorgeous blonde named Babette, who later became my gorgeous wife! And I was able to pay cash for our honeymoon, which was a luxury cruise to Caribbean islands like St. Kitts, St. Lucia and Barbados.

THIS IS HOW I WENT FROM BASEMENT TO BESTSELLER TO BARBADOS IN JUST 24 MONTHS.

Which means, as a result of following the 7-Figure Expert Formula I'll teach you in this book, I went from basement to bestseller to Barbados in just 24 months.

I've also generated over $31 million in online sales,and helped my clients add over $2.8 Billion in found revenues— meaning, I've helped my clients add six, and seven and even eight figures to their business in record time while winning their lives back.

Now, The Bad News

That's the good news. Now here's the bad news: *I had to spend over $750,000.00 and more than 20 years to figure all this out.* Here's what that means for you:

1. You don't have to go through the pain, torment and agony that I did in order to get all this in place.

You're welcome!

2. You have hidden equity in your business right now.

3. The longer you wait to get this in place working for you, *the more money, opportunity and freedom will slip through your fingers.*

THE MORE YOU DELAY, THE MORE YOU'LL PAY.

That's the bad news. However, the GOOD news is that we've seen my 7-Figure Expert Formula work for...

- Doctors

- Dentists

- Chiropractors

- B2B Consultants

- Internet Marketers

- Course creators

- Authors

- Speakers

- Network marketers

- Coaches

- Nurses

- Health professionals

- Affiliate marketers

- Real estate investors

- Anyone who wants to start, grow or scale any business!

Here's What This Isn't

Let me be very clear—here's what this ISN'T. This is NOT about:

- Crypto

- MLM

- Bitcoin

- Get rich quick

- Facebook ads

- Webinars

- Hustle and grind

And the GREAT news is that anybody can do this...

- WITHOUT having a product

- WITHOUT having "followers"

- WITHOUT spending a dime on ads

- WITHOUT having any special skills

- WITHOUT a fancy degree

- WITHOUT working an insane amount

- ANY country in the world

- ANY age (old or young)

- ANY background

- ALL YOU NEED is a laptop an Internet connection

Sound good? I hope you're as excited to learn this as I am to teach it to you!

It Ain't What You Don't Know…

Will Rogers once said, "It ain't what a man don't know that gets him in trouble. It's what he knows that ain't so." In our modern language, that quote might read as follows:

It's not what a person doesn't know that gets them in trouble. It's what they think they know that simply isn't true.

Let me give you an example. For tens of thousands of years, human beings believed that the Earth was flat. Because you walk outside, walk around, and you can see that, of course it's flat.

Then some Greeks like Pythagoras and Eratosthenes came along and said, "Uh guys, I hate to tell you this, but I can prove that the Earth is round." And of course they were roundly ridiculed for voicing their beliefs.

Another example: for tens of thousands of years, humans thought that the sun goes around the Earth. Just go outside, look around and you can tell that obviously, the sun's going around the Earth.

Then a guy named Galileo comes along and says, "Uh guys, I hate to tell you this, but I can prove that the Earth is going around the Sun." And of course, they threw him in jail for voicing his beliefs.

See what I mean? So the question I have for you today is: *How many things do you "know" that simply "ain't so?"*

Are You Ready For A Real Breakthrough?

This is the question I have for you today: *Are you ready for a real breakthrough?* Because I'm going to share some things in this book that might blow you away; might cause you to question what you think you know; and even say, *"I never thought of it that way."*

So, are you ready for a real breakthrough? I hope the answer is a resounding YES NOAH!

Let's go!

CHAPTER 2

Phase One: 7-Figure Beliefs

"Dare to dream! What you believe to be possible will always come to pass, to the extent that you deem it possible. It really is as simple as that."
—Anton St. Maarten

B efore we dive into my 7-Figure Expert Formula, I have a very important question for you...

Why Did You Start Your Own Business?

Here are some of the most common answers I get from my clients when I ask this question:

- I'm unemployable.

- I don't like punching a time clock for a boss.

- I want the freedom to be of service to more people.

- I like helping people.

- I want to work on my own terms.

- To earn more money.

- To have my money grow and work for me.

- To have a better livelihood.

- To be able to travel wherever and whenever I want.

- To make a difference.

- To help other people escape the rat race.

Can you relate to any of these?

Why Aren't You Living The Freedom Lifestyle Yet?

As my company, SuccessClinic.com, we teach that the main reason that people start their own business is **the desire to live a Freedom Lifestyle.**

Now, what does that mean? It means that YOU get to do the things that you want, when you want, with whom you want. That's the basic definition of a Freedom Lifestyle.

For example, some of the things we get to do are jet skiing, swimming with dolphins, going on cruises with family and friends, and frankly, have a lot of fun.

So my next question is:

If that's where you want to be, why aren't you there yet?

THIS IS WHY YOU STARTED YOUR BUSINESS.

Here are some of the most common answers I get from my clients when I ask this question:

- Head trash.

- I don't believe in myself.

- I haven't found the right coach.

- Wrong mindset.

- Lack of systems.
- Lack of money.
- Lack of time.

How Many of These Can You Relate To?

Here are some of the most common symptoms I see when people hire me to coach them, whether 1:1 or in a group setting:

1. Constantly worrying about money and finances.
2. Difficulty paying bills and meeting financial obligations.
3. Struggling to save for the future or afford luxuries.
4. Feeling stressed and overwhelmed by financial pressure.
5. Feeling stuck and unable to make changes or improvements in your business.
6. Working long hours but still falling behind or not making progress.
7. Feeling stuck in a rut and unable to try new things or take risks
8. Difficulty attracting and retaining customers or clients
9. Lack of motivation and feeling burned out
10. Struggling to take time off or disconnect from work
11. Constantly thinking about work and finding it difficult to relax or enjoy your personal time
12. Struggling to pay yourself a reasonable salary

13. Experiencing negative impacts on physical and mental health due to financial stress.

14. Struggling to make decisions or prioritize tasks

15. Lacking focus and direction

16. Wasting valuable time and resources on unimportant jobs

17. Struggling to attract and retain customers or clients

18. Lack of motivation and drive

19. Low productivity and efficiency

20. You don't have a clear action plan to reach your goals and fulfill your dreams.

FACT: These are all symptoms. They are NOT the real problem.

Of course, all of these symptoms lead to other problems; however, they are not the actual problem. Now another word for symptom is *pain*. Which means that you may be experiencing one or more of these symptoms, and that's going to show up in your life as pain.

For example, imagine you have a toothache and your tooth really hurts. That pain really disrupts your whole day, doesn't it? Because when you have a toothache, you can't really function that well. So your focus becomes, *I gotta get rid of this pain.*

So you make an appointment with the dentist and the dentist examines your tooth and says, "Yep, you've got a cavity there. Okay, next!"

And you're like, "Wait, what? You just told me what's

causing my pain. But now I need you to FIX it!

Now imagine that this dentist says, "Okay, here's a prescription for some painkillers. Take these painkillers and you won't feel the pain so much."

Does that sound like a good solution to you? Of course not! Because all that would happen is that you'd be masking the pain somewhat. However, the ACTUAL problem has not been fixed, which is that you have a cavity that is causing you a lot of pain.

What would a GOOD dentist do? Naturally, a good dentist will recommend a more comprehensive treatment protocol, such as a dental filling, dental crown, dental bonding or even root canal therapy, that will fix the *actual* problem and thereby cause your pain to disappear.

What A Good Coach Does vs. What Other Coaches Do

Most coaches and gurus out there are focused on the pain, the symptom. As a result, they recommend band-aid approaches that might mask the pain somewhat, but that don't fix the actual, underlying cause of the pain.

When you only treat symptoms without fixing the underlying cause of the pain, what inevitably happens to the symptoms? Exactly: the symptoms come back, except they usually come back even more—as a result, you're going to experience even more pain, because you never got the underlying cause of the pain fixed.

THIS IS WHAT A GREAT COACH GIVES YOU.

What I'm giving you in this book and what I've been teaching my clients since 1997 is a proven, step-by-step, paint-by-numbers formula that *fixes the root problem of all the symptoms I mentioned above.*

Would You Be Okay With Hockey Stick Growth?

In this book, I'll give you several examples of how my clients have achieved what we like to call "hockey stick growth." What does hockey stick growth mean?

Imagine if your business has been going along like this...

In other words, you're working hard, you're working long hours, and you've tried a lot of things, but your income basically stays the same month after month, year after year.

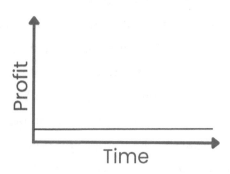

Well, what if somebody comes along and gives you something that fixes the underlying problem and you get hockey stick growth. That looks something like this...

Now if you'd like to see hockey stick growth in YOUR business, like we see over and over and over again with my

clients, get ready—because that's what this book is all about!

This Is The Real Problem You're Facing

Now that you understand the underlying philosophy and why what I do is different, let me show you what the real problem is. The real problem is **_Income Ceiling Syndrome._**

Let me show you what I mean. Prior to figuring all this out, I was poor. (You can say that I was broke or not abundant, or whatever you want to say. The fact is, I was poor.) Remember, I grew up poor in a rich neighborhood. And if I hadn't spent all that time and money working on myself, I'd probably still be poor, because that was how I was raised.

Now I live a life that, by any standards, is an abundant life. But it wasn't easy and it took a long time—much longer than I would have liked. However, the main reason it took so long for me is because I paid all those gurus all that money, only to find out they suck at teaching and coaching!

As you read this book, you might have thoughts come up like, "I can't do it" or "I can't afford it" and the like. These type of thoughts are what I call "poor Noah thinking."

What's the opposite of that type of thinking? What I like to call "Abundant Noah Thinking." I want you to catch yourself every time you have a "poor Noah" thought, and switch it to an "Abundant Noah" thought.

Because if I can do it, you can do it too! If I can get hockey stick growth in my business, and if I've helped so many other people do it, that means you can do it, too!

Therefore, catch yourself as you read this book and say, "Am I thinking like poor Noah? Or am I thinking like Abundant Noah?"

The Freedom Lifestyle Formula

A moment ago, I mentioned that the main reason most people start their own business is to have a Freedom Lifestyle. But what does that actually mean?

IF I CAN DO IT, YOU CAN DO IT TOO.

What I realized—and this is what I work with my clients on every day, and have been for more than 25 years now—is that a Freedom Lifestyle consists of four elements. These four elements are **time, energy, relationships, and money.**

When you have those four elements working in concert, you have what we like to call a Freedom Lifestyle.

What's Your Freedom Temperature?

When you go to the doctor's office (like I was saying earlier about going to the dentist), you're probably visiting the doctor

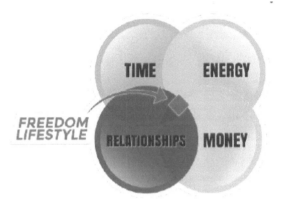

because you have some kind of pain. In general, you don't go to the doctor when you're feeling great, right? Generally speaking, you go to the doctor when something's hurt, when you have pain, when something's not right.

When you go to the doctor, what's the first thing that doctor does? They take your temperature. So what I'd like you to do now is ***take your freedom temperature.***

While this exercise only takes a few minutes, it's really going to be important as we go through this book. So be sure to do it!

Here's what I want you to do. I'm going to give you four statements, and I want you to rate yourself on a scale from one to 10; where one means you totally disagree with the statement, and 10 means you totally agree with the statement. Got it?

Here's your statement for **Time Freedom:**

"My business and personal life are balanced. My free time is totally free from the business, and I have enough scheduled and protected focused time to work with my best opportunities."

THIS IS HOW TO TAKE YOUR FREEDOM TEMPERATURE.

Rate yourself from 1-10 based on whether you totally agree with this statement (10) to you totally disagree with this statement (1).

Next, here's your statement for **Energy Freedom:**

"I am freed up to work on only what I'm good at and love to do, and freed from things I'm not good at and dislike doing."

Rate your level of agreement from 1-10 on this statement.

Next, here's your statement for **Relationship Freedom:**

"I'm leveraged by my team to work only with my best clients and top opportunities, and my personal relationships are healthy and supportive."

Rate your level of agreement from 1-10 on this statement.

Finally, here's your statement for **Money Freedom:**

"My company's profitability gives us room to invest in our growth on our team, and I have enough money to do the things I want when I want to do them."

Isn't that why you're in business—to turn a profit so that you can invest in your own personal growth and the things you enjoy?

Now, add those four numbers together and you'll get a number between four and 40. Meaning, if your total is four, you rated yourself a one in all four areas. If you gave yourself a perfect 10 in all areas, your score would be 40.

What is YOUR freedom temperature?

Do You Need Emergency Care?

If you're visiting the doctor because you're in pain, you'd want the doctor to give it to you straight, right? You wouldn't want him to beat around the bush. You'd rather he gets right to the point and tell you what you need to know.

Well, I'm the doctor in this scenario, since you came to me because something's not quite right in your life. So let me give it to you straight.

If your Freedom Lifestyle Score is under 20, we need to get you to the ICU. That means this is an emergency. That means you need some help, and you need it right now. Is that fair to say?

If you scored between 20 to 30, you're doing well, but you still might want to get some outside help, because there's still room for improvement

IF THIS IS YOUR FREEDOM SCORE, GET HELP RIGHT AWAY.

And if you scored over 30, congratulations! You're doing well, and perhaps you might need a few tweaks here and there.

As the doctor/coach, I can tell you that most people who take this test when they come to me score below 25. Which means, don't panic! Help is right here.

In fact, after coaching thousands of clients over the last two decades plus, I've identified what I call *the 5 Root Causes of Income Ceiling Syndrome.* While that sounds like a mouthful, the great news for YOU is that if you get any ONE of these problems fixed, you can experience **hockey stick growth** in your business in record time!

Who Do You Think You Are?

Before we examine the 5 Root Causes, let's look at where you are (and who you are) right now and who and where you want to be.

Where you are right now is what I call your **Current Limited Identity.** This is *who you think you are right now.* I also call that the Now You.

Remember that Will Rogers quote I told you about? Based on my experience, right now you are believing things about yourself that simply aren't true.

For example, you may believe that you can't be a 7-Figure Expert because you don't have the time; you don't have the money; you can't afford it; you're too old; you've made too many mistakes, and so on. These are just a few examples that people tell me before they start 1:1 or group coaching with me. That's your Current Limited Identity, the

Now You—who you think you are right now.

However, for over 25 years now, I've been helping people move from their Current Limited Identity (CLI) to their New Desired Identity, or NDI. That's your pot of gold at the end of the rainbow.

Notice that I'm already helping you paint a picture of this in your mind. As you move through this book, I'm going to show you how to go from your CLI (what you believe about yourself right now) to your NDI (who you want to be—your pot of gold).

What's the main reason you are where you are, and not where you want to be? Psychologists call this *cognitive dissociative conditioning*. However, more than two decades ago, I coined a much easier term: ***Head trash.***

Common Symptoms of Head Trash

You could say that I've written more than 20 books about this one topic: How to take out your head trash. So let's look at some of the most common symptoms of head trash:

- Procrastination
- Low self esteem
- Lack of self confidence
- Negative self talk
- Limiting beliefs
- Difficulty making decisions
- Fear of failure or rejection
- Perfectionism
- Difficulty managing time or setting priorities
- Difficulty taking action or falling through on plans
- Hard to manage stress or life's challenges
- Trouble setting and achieving goals
- Hard time finding meaning or purpose in life
- Difficulty feeling fulfilled or satisfied with life
- Struggling to maintain a healthy work-life balance
- Struggling with finding or pursuing your passion
- Difficulty finding happiness or contentment.

Many of these symptoms are very subtle, which is why many people aren't aware of the root problem. Speaking of which, if you would have asked me before I discovered my Afformations® Method and success anorexia in 1997, I'd have told you that I related to every one of these symptoms. Why do you think I decided to commit suicide back then? In fact, I struggled with each of these symptoms before I discovered my iconic formula.

Here's What Won't Fix The Problem

While most people aren't even aware of the problem, let alone how to fix it, let me share with you what WON'T fix this underlying problem that's causing all your other problems:

- Ignoring it or hoping it will go away on its own

- Trying to suppress or push down negative thoughts and feelings.

- Believing in head trash is a permanent part of your identity.

- "Shelf-help" books or online courses.

- Seeking quick fixes or shortcuts rather than addressing the root causes.

- Vision boards

- Years of therapy.

- Watching YouTube videos for hours on end.

- Working harder and longer without a proven, plug-and-play SOLUTION that fixes the real problem.

How many of these have you tried?

Top 10 Head Trashes That No Longer Serve You

These are commonly-held beliefs that many people believe,

that will no longer serve you:

1. "I'm not capable of overcoming my head trash."
2. "I don't have the time or resources to work on taking out my head trash."
3. "I'm too old to change."
4. "My head trash is a permanent part of me and I just have to live with it."
5. "I'm not worthy or deserving of overcoming my head trash."
6. "I don't have the willpower or discipline to make changes."
7. "I don't have the support or resources I need to overcome my head trash."
8. "I'm too stuck in my ways to change."
9. "I'm too afraid of failure or rejection."
10. "Seeking help is a sign of weakness."

Do you believe any of these?

Do you think these would fall under "poor Noah" thinking or "Abundant Noah" thinking?

Right—these are all examples of "poor Noah" thinking, and that's why these are examples of head trashes that no longer serve you and that you must take out immediately.

How Much Is Your Head Trash Costing You Right Now?

This is a very, very important question: ***If you don't take out your head trash, how much do you think it's going to cost*** *you over the next 12 months?*

I want you to get a real number in your head as you read this. In fact, make a written note right now of the amount of money it's going to cost you if you DON'T take out your head trash in the next 12 months.

Let me give you a real-life example. I ask this question of every one of my clients, whether we're doing 1:1 or group coaching. I was talking with one of my clients named Charles.

I said, "Charles, how much do you think it's going to cost you over the next 12 months if you don't get this problem fixed, if we don't take out your head trash?"

Without batting an eye, he replied, "It's going to cost me a million dollars. Noah, if I don't take out my head trash the next 12 months, I'm going to lose out on a million dollars."

I said, "Believe it or not, I hear this every day. It's very common. So I tell you what. Just give me 10% of that million dollars, and I'll find you that million dollars in the next 12 months."

THIS PIECE ALONE WAS COSTING HIM A MILLION DOLLARS A YEAR.

"In other words," I said, "If you give me one dollar and I give you 10 dollars back, is that a good deal?"

He said, "Yes, that's a very good deal."

So he did. He paid me ten percent of a million dollars, which is $100,000, to coach him one-on-one. And guess what happened?

I didn't find Charles a million dollars in the next 12 months.

I found him $1.8 million dollars in just 10 months!

In other words, because of my coaching, I found him nearly two million dollars that he would not have had if he hadn't followed my advice and taken out his head trash. Talk about hockey stick growth!

Not only that, but because I helped him win his life back, Charles bought a new RV and went on a seven-week vacation with his wife. He told me that not only was he making more money than ever, he also had more TIME than ever. Talk about a win-win-win!

The One Problem That's Causing All Your Other Problems

In fact, your head trash is the one problem that's causing all your other problems. Which is precisely why we start with taking out your head trash.

I want you to imagine we start working together today, right now. And I give you everything that you need to reach your pot of gold at the end of the rainbow, to take out your head trash and become the New You.

Now imagine that we're having this conversation 12 months from now. *What would have happened in your life for you to be happy with your progress?*

Take out your notes and write about what your life looks like, once we've taken out your head trash. What does it look like for you? Are you spending more time with your family?

Are you making more money, and you have more time off? Maybe you're taking vacations that you haven't taken in a long time or ever? Have you retired your spouse so you can travel together? Are you spending more time with your grandkids?

Paint a very clear picture of YOUR pot of gold, because your life can change in the next 12 weeks, let alone the next 12 months, if you're open to the possibility.

Phase One: 7-Figure Beliefs

As you can now see, Phase One of my 7-Figure Expert Formula is **7-Figure Beliefs.** This means that you're no longer coming from "poor you" (your Current Limited Identity) and you start coming from "Abundant You" (your New Desired Identity).

For example, here are some common head trashes that you need to take out immediately.

HEAD TRASH: "Noah, this all sounds great, but I just don't have the time to do this."

To combat this very common head trash, I invented what I call The 5-minute Belief Shift. Here's how it works.

I created iAfform® Audios, which are downloadable audio recordings that you can listen to anytime, anywhere, that change your subconscious thought patterns while you're not even paying attention.

For instance, you can put your iAfform® Audios on your phone or laptop and listen to them throughout your day, while you're doing other things. What's amazing about iAfform Audios is that they reprogram your subconscious thought patterns on autopilot. So much for that head trash!

HEAD TRASH: "This sounds amazing, but I'm worried that I won't see any progress or results."

Here's what Aubrey, one of my clients, says about coaching with me:

> "When I first attended a Noah St. John event, I came thinking, 'How can Noah figure out things about me, I'm different than anyone else and I don't think these things will come up.' But the things Noah says bring up ideas and thoughts in your mind to where you learn that much more about yourself.
>
> Now everybody comes from different walks of life, different businesses, different issues, different things that they're stuck in, different head trash as Noah calls it. And he has a way of engaging everybody. It doesn't matter where you're stuck, I'm able to learn more

and grow more. Before you even realize it, he's taught you how to make more money and you don't even realize how it happened! I know that happened with me. And it was simply before I even really started working his habits into my business, it was really getting rid of the head trash as he teaches. And as I did that, **within a year, my business income that I had actually had for 15 years had DOUBLED** simply by incorporating the habits that Noah teaches.

The fact is, there's no better time than right now. It seems inconvenient initially, but then once you've done it, you're like, 'I can't imagine having had missed that and not having that peace in my life.'"

Have you heard of the phrase "working yourself to death?" Well, Aubrey had actually been doing that before she came to me. It's true: she told me that she had been working at 100 or more hours every week for *15 years.* 15 years!

She was working so hard that she actually ended up in a wheelchair, and her doctors told her that she might never walk again. They told her that she had to stop working so hard.

SHE WAS LITERALLY WORKING HERSELF TO DEATH.

But she couldn't stop, because she was on this treadmill and just working, working, working all the time.

When she first came to one of my events, she was at her lowest point. Yet because of my coaching and her implementation, **she doubled her income in just 12 months, after 15 years of nearly working herself to death.**

Many people will read Aubrey's story and the other case studies in this book or on my website and say to themselves, "Sure, they did it, but it won't work for me."

What does that sound like to you? Exactly: *More head trash!*

So I want you to reverse that right now. Instead of believing that old head trash, I want you to start saying this:

If they did it, why not me?

Let me ask you a question: Is it ridiculous to think that just one thing I've taught you so far in this book could help you get better results in the next 12 weeks?

I hope you agree that it's not ridiculous at all. In fact, it's perfectly logical, right?

Here's All You Need to Succeed

The only three things you need to succeed are...

1. The Right PLAN (What to do)
2. The Right TOOLS (How to do it)
3. The Right SUPPORT (The people who believe in

you)

You see, building your dream business and your dream lifestyle is like building your dream home. First, you need *the right PLAN:* the blueprint you're going to follow.

In my one-on-one and group coaching programs, that's the paint-by-numbers, fill-in-the-blanks, plug-and-play systems, templates, resources, and strategies that have made me and my clients billions over the last two decades plus.

Then you need *the right TOOLS* that enable you to actually build the business or lifestyle you desire.

Finally, you need *the right SUPPORT.* You need the person or people in your corner believing in you—oftentimes, before you even believe in yourself!

In my coaching programs, we call these The Three Pillars of Transformation: the right plan, the right tools, and the right support so you reach your pot of gold faster than you ever could by working alone.

Let me end this chapter with a quote from Denzel Washington:

"I've found that nothing in life is worthwhile unless you take risks. Nothing. Nelson Mandela said, 'There is no passion to be found playing small and settling for a life that's less than the one you're capable of living' Without consistency, you'll never finish. So do what you feel passionate about. Take chances. Don't be afraid to fail big, to dream. But remember, dreams without goals are just dreams."

Let me add that a goal without ACTION is just a dream. That means, you can have all the big dreams in the world—

but if you don't take action, nothing will happen!

Now let's go to Phase Two of my 7-Figure Expert Formula...

CHAPTER 3
Phase Two: 7-Figure Habits

"Sow a thought, reap an action; sow an action, reap a habit; sow a habit, reap a character; sow a character, reap a destiny."
—Stephen R. Covey

Now let's examine the next cause of Income Ceiling Syndrome. Remember, the great news for YOU is that if you get any ONE of these problems fixed, you can experience **hockey stick growth** in your business!

I want you to consider the fact that the gurus and hustle and grinders are all focused on "pushing you harder." For instance, all the motivational speakers and gurus are telling you to work, work, work all the time and keep your nose to the grindstone.

However, more than 20 years ago, I coined a different term called *The Foot On The Brake Syndrome.* What does that mean?

I want you to imagine that wealth or financial freedom or success or happiness (whatever term you'd like to use) is a destination. In fact, wealth IS destination that you want to reach.

Now, if you want to reach your destination, one way that you get there is through a vehicle, right? Believe it or not, there are only four vehicles that we can use to get to the destination called Wealth.

The four Wealth Vehicles are:

1. Your retirement account (your 401K, IRA, etc.)

2. Real estate

3. Investments (stocks, bonds, securities, etc.)

4. Your own business

Now "a job" is not on this list because it is uncommon for a person to become wealthy by working at a job. Not that it can't be done, but it's definitely not common for a job to enable you to reach that destination called Wealth.

After coaching countless thousands people to reach the destination called Wealth, they have all used a combination of these vehicles. So let me ask you: Which of these vehicles are YOU currently using to get to that destination called Wealth?

Are You Driving With One Foot on The Brake?

Here's the point: You can be using all of these vehicles right now, or you can be using one, two or three. However, if you're driving down the road of life with one foot on the brake, you're simply not going to reach the destination called Wealth.

Let's say you want to take a trip, and let's say you've got a nice, reliable car that you really enjoy driving. So you start down the highway towards your destination. You're thinking positive, you're motivated, and you can't wait to get there.

So you press down really hard on the gas pedal. But unbeknownst to you, at the same time you have one foot on the gas, your other foot is on the brake.

So here you are driving down the highway of life trying to reach your destination, but you have one foot on the brake. How long do you think it's going to take you to reach your destination? Exactly: along, long, long time!

So let's say Guru #1 sees that you're having a problem, and they say to you, *"You know what you need? You need a more expensive type of gas. That's your problem!"*

HERE'S WHAT THE GURUS DO THAT SCREWS US UP.

So you pull into the gas station and fill your tank with the most expensive, high-octane gas you can find, and you get back on the highway of life.

But guess what? Because no one told you what the real problem is, you've still got one foot on the brake, so you're still not making much progress.

Then Guru #2 says, *"You know what you need? You should get a new set of tires. Try these really expensive tires. That's your problem."*

So you go to the service station, spend more of your hard-earned money buying the most expensive tires they've got, and you get back on the highway of life. But guess what—you've still got one foot on the brake, so you're still not reaching your destination.

Finally, Guru #3 says, *"You know what you need? You should get a new car! This car isn't good enough, you should get a really expensive new sports car like I've got. That's your problem."*

So you reluctantly trade in your nice, reliable car, spend a ton of your hard-earned money buying an expensive new sports car, and thinking positively—but with a lot less than your bank account—get back on the highway of life.

Yet even after all this time, money and effort that you've spent...

Because no one took the time to show you the real problem, which was simply that your foot was on the brake... You end up not reaching your goals, not fulfilling your destiny, and end up feeling so frustrated that you give up on your dream.

So let me ask you a question. If buying more expensive gas, more expensive tires, and even a brand new car isn't going to get you where you want to go, shouldn't you do whatever it takes to get your foot off the brake?

Bottom line, if your foot is on the brake, you simply won't reach your destination, and you'll end up spending and wasting a ton of time, money and effort not getting where you want to go. So really, when you look at it, getting your foot off the brake is the key to getting everything that you want in life.

Common Symptoms of Foot On The Brake Syndrome

- Not making enough money to justify all the hard work and long hours you're putting in

- Constant self-criticism

- Negative thoughts about your own abilities

- Believing you're not good enough.

- Dismissing your own achievements

- Comparing yourself negatively to others

- Feeling like nothing will ever change

- Settling for the crumbs of life

Can you relate to any of these?

Here's What Won't Fix The Problem

While most people aren't even aware of the problem, let alone how to fix, here's what WON'T fix the problem:

- Ignoring it or hoping it will fix itself

- Trying to cover it up or hide it

- Procrastinating or avoiding action

- Blaming other people

- Believing you're stuck with it

- More shelf-help

- Believing you don't have the time or the resources to change

- Believing you're not worthy of happiness or success

- Working harder and longer without a proven, paint-by-numbers SOLUTION that fixes the real problem

How many of these have you tried?

How Much Is This Costing You?

This is another very important question: ***How much will it cost you in the next 12 months if you don't get your foot off the brake?***

Now, let me ask you this: ***Would you rather get this problem fixed sooner or later?*** I hope your answer is sooner, rather than later.

Remember, the media companies want to keep you stuck and in fear, because it's more profitable for them to keep you addicted to those media. Their job is to keep you addicted, because that's where their profits are. Don't let them do that to you anymore, because *the more you postpone, the less you'll own.*

Your Inner Game and Outer Game

Your *Inner Game* is everything that happens between your ears that you can't see directly, but that affects everything you do. Your *Outer Game* is everything that you can see directly, because it's right in front of you.

Did you know that 90% of your success is based on your Inner Game? When I help my clients add six, seven and eight figures in record time, 90% of that hockey stick growth happens when people master their Inner Game.

Of course, you have to master your Outer Game too—however, my 7-Figure Expert Formula is based on more than 25 years of experience helping my one-on-one and group coaching clients add billions of dollars in found revenues.

Your Inner Game is the foundation of everything that we're going to be doing together. and if you don't master your Inner Game, it doesn't matter how many seminars you go to, how many books you read— none of that will make much difference.

YOUR INNER GAME DETERMINES 90% OF YOUR SUCCESS.

That's why I created my two flagship online courses—the first is called **Power Habits® Academy,** my foundational Inner Game program that has helped thousands of people around the world. The second is my foundational Outer Game program called **7-Figure Machine**, because my clients were begging me to teach them how to make money online.

For example, I want you to write your #1 problem, challenge or frustration in your life and business right now. Then list five ways that not having this problem fixed is costing you in time, energy, relationships and money. Remember, those are the four elements of my freedom Lifestyle Formula.

Then I want you to write whether you think this is an Inner Game or Outer Game problem. I'll bet that 90% of the problem you think you have is really an Inner Game problem.

Phase Two: 7-Figure Habits

Phase Two of my 7-Figure Expert Formula is **7-Figure Habits**. This means that you stop driving down the road of life with one foot on the brake, and stop stopping yourself from the level of success you're capable of.

For example, you may be thinking this:

HEAD TRASH: "Noah, this sounds amazing, but I'm not convinced this will work for me."

Here's what my clients Ed and Karen have to say...

Karen: "I was the skeptic coming into this because I'm really not very coachable. But after just ONE coaching session with Noah, we had some wonderful breakthroughs on how we can really kick start our business" Because **he gave us several different options on multiple streams of income,** which we wholeheartedly believe in. Noah is very straightforward, and told us that this is what you have to do to be successful. And that type of talking to me and kicking me in the butt, is just what I need. And I haven't been able to find that in anyone else but Noah."

Ed: "There are so many trainers and coaches that hit pieces and parts that don't complete the circle. But **Noah covers everything from mindset to funnels to marketing to any piece that you need.** He has the whole thing, and then gives you step-by-step guidance and direction. So it really is the complete package with Noah!"

HEAD TRASH: "I'm scared to try and fail."
Here's what my client Tim T. has to say...

"I hired Noah St. John to coach me when I was at a time in my life where I was kind of looking for what was next. I had retired from a successful business and I thought I wanted to take one path. But after getting coaching with Noah, I knew that I had a really big dream that I wasn't going after, out of fear. After coaching with Noah, I knew that I had the ability to live that dream. So I started this new business and built it into a million-dollar business within two years. So if you get a chance to get coached by Noah, I promise that it'll change your life like it changed mine."

Can you say hockey stick growth?

These are just a few examples of what can happen when you start using my 7-Figure Habits System. For example, many people have spent a lot of money on all the marketing gurus out there, yet they're still stuck. Why?

It's because those guys never really address Inner Game—or if they do, they only give it lip service. They only talk about the surface, or symptom level. That's one reason that my clients get hockey stick growth—because what I do is different from what those guys are doing.

That's also why I give you my fill-in-the-blank, paint-by-numbers formula to master your Inner Game and take out your head trash in a very systematic way, so you can finally get your foot off the brake and reach the level of success you're perfectly capable of.

Now let's go to Phase Three of my 7-Figure Expert Formula...

CHAPTER 4

Phase Three: 7-Figure Offers

*"Education is the key to unlock the
golden door of freedom."*
—George Washington Carver

Now let's examine the next cause of Income Ceiling
Syndrome. Remember, the great news for YOU is that if
you get any ONE of these problems fixed, you can experience
hockey stick growth in your business!

Many entrepreneurs and experts are constantly
distracted by "shiny object syndrome." That's because there
are an infinite number of distractions that can take your focus
off your core work.

However, the real issue for most entrepreneurs is
Inferior Offer Disorder. Now, what does that mean?

Common Symptoms of Inferior Offer Disorder (IOD)

- Procrastination or hesitation when it comes to making offers

- Difficulty setting prices or fees for your products or services

- Fear of failure or rejection when making an offer

- Lack of confidence in your products or services

- Difficulty communicating the value or benefits of your product or service

- Trouble handling rejections or negotiating terms

- Struggle when closing a sale or securing a contract

- Difficulty setting and enforcing boundaries with customers or clients

Can you relate to any of these?

Here's What Won't Fix The Problem

While most people aren't even aware of the problem, let alone how to fix it, here's what WON'T fix this problem:

- Pretending the problem doesn't exist.

- Ignoring it and hoping it will go away on its own.

- Believing that you're simply incapable of success.

- Seeking quick fixes or shortcuts rather than addressing the root cause of the problem.

- Getting bogged down by negative thinking or self doubt

- Wishing and hoping the problem will somehow fix itself.

- Working harder and longer without a proven, connect-the-dots FORMULA that fixes the REAL problem.

How many of these have you tried?

How Much Is This Costing You?

This is another very important question: How much will it cost you in the next 12 months if you don't get your IOD problem fixed?

Now, let me ask you this: Would you rather get this problem fixed sooner or later? I hope your answer is sooner, rather than later.

Remember, the marketing gurus want you stuck and confused, because it's more profitable for them to keep you dependent on them. Don't let them push you around any longer, because the longer you wait, the greater the weight..

Phase Three: 7-Figure Offers

Phase Three of my 7-Figure Expert Formula is **7-Figure Offers.** This means creating Irresistible Offers that attract your Ideal buyers like bees to honey, so you can stop putting in so much effort without seeing the return on investment you want.

Let's start with a key question: What is an Irresistible Offer? An Irresistible Offer is **90% Transformation + 10% Service Delivery.**

What do I mean by that? First, let's ask this deeper question: Why make offers in the first place?

Because people don't want more information. Today, they crave TRANSFORMATION.

Does information alone create change? Of course not. Information alone does not create change, because if information alone created change, everyone would be rich, happy and thin!

Imagine if you wanted to make more money in your online business. You go to YouTube and type in "how to make money in my online business." What happens? Right—you get 350 million billion kajillion videos of every clown out there telling you how to make money online.

THIS IS WHY INFORMATION ALONE DOES NOT CREATE CHANGE.

What are you supposed to do with that? Most people will watch only the most popular results, the ones with the most views. However, isn't it also true that the most popular guys out there are often the WORST teachers?

Which means that popularity and goodness of teaching usually has an inverse ratio—in other words, the more popular the guru is, usually the WORSE teacher they are.

What if you want to lose weight and have six pack abs.

You go to YouTube and search "how to have six-pack abs." Again, $10 million billion kajillion results, right? So why isn't everyone rich, happy and thin?

Because there's no *implementation* of information. What I often tell my clients, whether in our one-on-one or group coaching sessions, is this:

Information without implementation Is failed transformation.

Therefore, in order to make Irresistible Offers, stop talking about your *information* and start talking your *transformation*. As I've often said, we don't live in the Information Age, we live in the Information Overload Age! Most people you talk to are on overload—therefore, there's no lack of information, but there's a definite lack of transformation. And lack of transformation comes from a lack of implementation.

The Three Levels of Irresistible Offers

The three levels of Irresistible Offers are:

- Done For You (Typical price points $25K - $100K+)

- Done With You ($5K - $25K)

- Do It Yourself ($100 - $2000)

For example, we offer Done For You Book Service, where we create your book from start to finish, and Done For You Funnel Building, where we build your High Ticket

Funnel, Book Funnel, or Event Funnel.

Examples of our Done With You packages include The 12-Week breakthrough group coaching program, and one-on-one high-level mentoring for entrepreneurs, experts and athletes who want to break through to higher levels of income, impact and achievement.

Examples of our Do it Yourself programs include Power Habits® Academy and 7-Figure Machine. See **https://ShopNoahStJohn.com** for our complete product suite.

The Three Irresistible Offer Questions

If you want to begin offering Irresistible Offers to increase your income and impact, begin by answering these three key questions:

1. Who is your target audience?

2. What problem do you solve for your target audience?

3. How will you deliver your transformation?

For example, here are just a few of the ways you can deliver your transformation:

- Book and ebooks
  (see **https://NoahStJohn.com/books**)

- Online courses
  (see **https://ShopNoahStJohn.com**)

- Keynote speeches
  (see **https://BookNoah.com**)

- Group Coaching
  (see **https://BreakthroughwithNoah.com**)

- One-on-one coaching
  (see **https://NoahMentor.com**)

In fact, if you don't know the answer to even ONE of these three crucial questions, you and your business will be (and remain) STUCK.

Which means, whether you do this on your own, or you choose to do together with me and my team—so you can ACCELERATE your results up to 10 times faster, with far less time, effort and stress—these are the steps you're going to need to take:

The Three Irresistible Offers Steps

Step One: What are the biggest problems your Ideal Buyer hungers to solve?

List all of the problems that you are solving for your Ideal Buyer.

Step Two: What specific results can someone get from working with you?

This is where you want to list the specific RESULTS that your Ideal Buyer can get from working with you or buying your program.

Step Three: Show your clients' Journey of Transformation.

This is where you want to list the specific RESULTS that your Ideal Buyer can get from working with you or buying your program.

As you're reading this, some more head trash may have come up for you. So let's address that right here and now!

HEAD TRASH: "I don't know where to start."

Here's what my clients Dr. Stacey and Dean have to say...

> Dr. Stacey: As members of Dr. Noah's Inner Circle coaching, when we completed our first VIP Coaching Sessions with Noah, he provided us with so many tools and resources that are absolutely phenomenal. Getting coached by Noah is definitely worth the effort, time and money spent. It has taken us so far forward in our future!
>
> Dean: And I was the skeptic, I wasn't sure how this was going to work. I felt like we came in with just a blank piece of paper and not really knowing where we were going. Just a few hours later, we left feeling like we had accomplished so much. And I feel after just a few short hours that we accomplished so much!
>
> Dr. Stacey: So true! And even though I'm not a techie person, Noah and his team built my book and sales funnel for me, and now I'm making money in my sleep. I highly recommend Noah's coaching for your life and business, **because he can take you to**

new heights faster that we ever thought possible. It's definitely worth the investment in yourself and you will receive tenfold what you put in!

This is an example of how you can show your clients' Journey of Transformation, so your Ideal Buyers can see how they too can benefit from what you have to offer.

By the way, Stacey had what she thought was an "impossible dream" — to take her family on a Grand Canyon vacation. She actually told me when we started working together that she'd be thrilled if we could help her to get there in five to seven YEARS.

We got her there in less than 18 months!

As a coach, there is nothing more satisfying than having your clients send you pictures of their dream vacation that YOU helped them to manifest. Therefore, share your clients' Journey of Transformation.

HEAD TRASH: "I'm not sure if I need a coaching program or if I can just figure it out on my own."

Here's what my client Stephen B. says...

My business is up to 800% since we got started working with Noah St. John! One of the reasons that we wanted to build an online business was so I could transition out of the consultant space and into our own online digital business where we're coaching and helping individuals around the world. Noah has a consistent brand across the board, from his online presence to his in-person presence. Everything that you're doing with Noah, it has the same message: You can do this! Simple and easy. Now, there is no silver bullet—but Noah gives you a step-by-step approach. And you know, without a doubt that you can do what you want to do if you follow his program.

Would you be okay with hockey stick growth like an 800% increase in just 12 weeks? And if your head trash is saying "it's not possible" — replace it with this:

If they did it, why not me?

This Is All You Need To Succeed

Remember, all you need is the right PLAN, the right TOOLS and the right SUPPORT.

I can give you the right PLAN (what to do), the right TOOLS (how to dot it) and the right SUPPORT (believing in you when you may not believe in yourself yet). However, there's one thing you must supply that I can't give you.

Let's say I'm the best personal trainer in the business and you hire me to get in shape. And you say, "Dr. Noah, can you give me the best workouts, teach me the best foods to eat and believe in me so I get in the best shape of my life?"

And I say, "Of course, I can do that."

Then you say, "Oh, and by the way, I also want you to do my sit ups for me, so I get six pack abs."

Wouldn't that be great if we could hire somebody else to do our sit ups for us so WE get six-pack abs? Unfortunately, I have not seen how to make that work yet.

However, what if I told you that if you just do 10% of what I teach you, you can get that hockey stick growth that I've been talking about and showing you examples of?

If You're Missing Any One of These...

- If you don't have the right PLAN, you'll stay STUCK.

- If you don't have the right TOOLS, you'll be OVERWHELMED.

- If you don't have the right SUPPORT, you'll feel ALONE.

- And if you don't take right ACTION, what will happen is...NOTHING.

Therefore, make sure you take ACTION on what I'm sharing with you in this book, so you can start to see the TRANSFORMATION you desire in your life and your business.

Now let's go to Phase Four of my 7-Figure Expert Formula...

CHAPTER 5

Phase Four: 7-Figure Funnels

"The future belongs to those who believe
in the beauty of their dreams."
— Eleanor Roosevelt

Now let's examine the next cause of Income Ceiling Syndrome. Remember, the great news for YOU is that if you get any ONE of these problems fixed, you can experience hockey stick growth in your business!

Most experts and entrepreneurs are worried about trying to make everything perfect. They're trying this and testing that, while still being distracted by every marketing fad and gimmick that comes down the pike.

However, the real issue here is what I call **Franken-Funnels.** What does that mean and how much is it costing you right now?

Common Symptoms of Franken-Funnels

- Poor conversions from website visitors to leads

- Low conversions from leads to customers

- Lack of engagement or interaction from website visitors

- Lack of clarity or focus in the sales funnel process

- Missing a high converting offer or call to action

- Your offers aren't converting

- You don't have a clear or compelling value proposition

- Lacking a money making lead magnet or opt in offer

- You don't have a systematic lead nurturing process

- You're now making enough money from the leads you're getting

- You don't have automatic consistent profits

Can you relate to any of these?

Here's What Won't Fix The Problem

While most people aren't even aware of the problem, let alone how to fix it, here's what WON'T fix this problem:

- Constantly checking on social media or email.

- Wasting time on tasks that are not high priority or high impact

- Getting caught up in perfectionism.

- Trying to do everything yourself, instead of delegating or outsourcing to other people.

- Getting caught up in analysis paralysis.

- Getting overwhelmed by the scope of the project and just giving up.

- Working harder and longer without the copy and paste, fill-in-the-blank templates, tools and strategies that fix the ACTUAL problem.

How many of these have you tried or are you currently doing right now?

How Much Is This Costing You?

This is another very important question: ***How much will it cost you in the next 12 months if you don't replace your FrankenFunnels?***

Now, let me ask you this: ***Would you rather get this problem fixed sooner or later?*** I hope your answer is sooner, rather than later.

Remember, the social media companies want to keep you addicted to their platforms, because it's more profitable for them to keep you on those platforms as long as possible so they can keep showing you advertising. Don't let them suck your life away any longer, because *the more you delay, the more you'll pay..*

Phase Four: 7-Figure Funnels

Because this problem is so pervasive and costing you so much money, Phase Four of my 7-Figure Expert Formula is **7-Figure Funnels**. This means creating Automated Funnels that bring in money while you sleep, so you can stop working so hard and stop trading hours for dollars, and instead live a life of time freedom, location freedom and financial freedom.

The fact is, most people aren't willing to do this, because they're afraid. They're afraid of failure. They're afraid of success. They're afraid of this, they're afraid of that.

Well, guess what? That's precisely the thing that I've been fixing for more than 25 year now. In fact, the very thing that is keeping you STUCK is the very thing that I've been fixing for more than a quarter century and helped my clients add six, seven and eight figures as a result.

Would you like to deconstruct my 7-Figure Automated Funnels so you can model the process for YOUR business?

What Is An Automated Sales Funnel?

An **automated sales funnel** is the path that people take to buy your Irresistible Offers. Are you starting to see how this is all coming together?

First, we started by taking out your head trash.

Then we installed Power Habits® so you can stop stopping yourself from success.

Then we created Irresistible Offers that attract your

Ideal Buyers like bees to honey.

Now, we're building Automated Sales Funnels so you can make money while you sleep.

Remember I told you that in order to win, you need the right PLAN , the right TOOLS, and the right SUPPORT. Before I show you my three main Automated Sales Funnels that bring in 80% of my income, let me show you the tools I had to deal with BEFORE:

> **SEE HOW THIS ALL WORKS TOGETHER TO CREATE YOUR FREEDOM LIFESTYLE?**

BEFORE (Really??)

Let me ask you: if you had to use this tool to manage your sales funnels, what would you be feeling when you got up in the morning and you had to stare at this on your computer? Stressed? Overwhelmed? Nightmare? Angry? To the point of giving up?

That's exactly how I felt when this was the only tool I had to run my online business. I found myself getting angrier and angrier, I had a short temper, I was snapping at my wife and she would say things like, "What is wrong with you? What are you so angry about?"

And I'd say, "This tool is just driving me crazy. It's overwhelming and I hate it!" Is it any wonder so many experts and entrepreneurs feel the same way? Sometimes you just want to throw your computer out the window, you want to just pull your hair out and just give up, right? Have you ever felt that way?

Here's Why This Is Great News for YOU

Because I've made everything so much faster and easier for you? Have you heard that saying, "Pioneers get all the arrows?" Well, I've got all the arrows in my back to prove it. So, you're welcome again!

Do you believe that you can help people with your knowledge, skills and life experience? I hope the answer is yes, because if you don't believe it, why should anyone else believe it?

Do you believe you have something valuable to offer the world?

Do you believe that you can make a valuable contribution using your knowledge, skills and life experience?

If the answer to these questions is YES, then I believe it's your moral obligation to offers that will help people with your knowledge, skills and life experience, to make the world a better place.

Take Out Your Head Trash About Selling

Did you know that the word *sell* comes from an old English word meaning "to serve?" Have you ever considered how much head trash people have around this whole concept of *selling* or *sales*?

Once you realize that to *sell* actually means *to serve*, maybe that will help you to alleviate some of your head trash about selling.

What if, instead of getting upset when someone makes an offer, you lean forward and say, "Wow, let me see how they're making this offer and see, maybe it's something that would benefit me!" Rather than crossing your arms and saying, "Oh, they're just trying to sell me something." What if you lean in and learn, instead of crossing your arms and rejecting it outright?

Dr. Noah's 7-Figure Automated Funnels

Whether you choose to figure this out all by yourself, or we do it together (the smarter and faster way) so you can ACCELERATE your results up to 10 times faster, with less time, effort and stress, these are the steps you're going to need to take.

These three Automated Funnels bring in 80% of my annual income. That means there's no get guesswork, no starting from scratch. This is battle tested over 25 years, selling online starting from nothing.

I told you earlier that I started in a 300-square-foot

basement apartment in 1997 with $800 and a book on HTML. I didn't have any of the tools that we have today. Fact is, it's so much easier for you than it ever was for me.

How I Turn $9 Into $42 on Autopilot

My first Automated Funnel is called the Free+Shipping Funnel. You can see how this funnel works and go through it yourself at **https://SendMeaBookNoah.com** with my book *Get Rid of Your Head Trash About Money*.

When people enter the funnel, they see that the book is free and they just have to cover a nominal shipping fee.

That means most people pay $9.95 for a book, which is a reasonable price for a book, right?

Then I have what's called an OTO, which stands for One-Time Offer. That means you have an offer that is related to the first thing they just bought.

In this case, I have what's called The Afformations Solution for Money, which sells for $99.00 and then a second OTO, which is my program Get Unstuck Now which sells for $297.00.

Notice that we started with your Irresistible Offer, and now we're putting it in a funnel so people can buy it from around the world. However, most experts and entrepreneurs are doing this totally backwards. They have no plan, they're just winging it and working really hard and not making the money they want.

And that is the way to frustration and stress and overwhelm and agony and pain, which is what I had to go through. So I want to save you all that pain, torment and agony.

The point is, rather than just getting $10 when someone comes in your funnel, now you're making an average of $42 when someone comes in your funnel. Would you rather make $9 or $42 **with exactly the same amount of effort?**

Are you starting to see why my clients get hockey stick growth? With just a few little tweaks, we went from ten dollars to forty dollars per customer, which is 400% growth.

How I Turn $22 Into $51 While I Sleep

My second Automated Funnel is called the Event Funnel. You can see an example of this at **https://7FigureExpertEvent.com** with my 7-Figure Expert Event (just one of the many virtual events I do).

Have you seen all these people doing online challenges? I've seen 28-day challenges, 21-day challenges, 7-day challenges, 5-day challenges, 3-day challenges. I've done live events, virtual events, three-day events, two-day events, one-day events. As a marketer, you always have to test new things and see which works best for you and your audience.

However, no matter the event, it's basically the same format. The beautiful thing is, once you have this dialed in, you just lather, rinse, repeat and do as many as you want, as often as you want. But you don't have to try to figure it out from scratch any more. How much time effort and stress does it take to figure it out from scratch? A lot, right?

Well, what if I just give you my plug-and-play, fill-in-the-blank, paint-by-numbers system? It certainly would shorten your learning curve!

So in this case, rather than making $22 per registrant, now I'm making $51 per registrant, simply by adding a few little tweaks. That means I just doubled my money with just a few simple additions. See the hockey stick growth?

How I Turn $10 Into $10,000 While Doing What I Love

Now this one I know some people won't believe, simply because the numbers are staggering, which means it's going to go up against some people's head trash about money. However, my third Automated Funnel is called the High-Ticket Application Funnel. You can see an example of this at **https://BreakthroughwithNoah.com**.

Now if you don't have a high-ticket offer ($5,000 or more), you are stuck at the low ticket level. Of course, there's nothing wrong with low ticket (typically $2,000 or below). However, do you see why, if all you have is low ticket, it's going to be hard for you to scale? It's hard to scale if you don't have a high-ticket offer, whether it's $5,000, $10,000, $50,000 or more.

Remember earlier I told you about my client Charles, who paid me $100,000 to coach him one-on-one? What I didn't tell you was that sale came from just ONE phone call.

That's right—it didn't take weeks or months to close the sale. That's because I made it clear in just one phone call the value of hiring me to coach him, and he said yes—and went on to get an 1,800% return on his investment!

So the question is, would you rather make $10 or $10,000? Another way to look at it is: If you want to scale to $1,000,000 per year, is it easier to sell 100,000 units at $10 per unit, or 100 units at $10,000 per unit?

Ironically, it's just as easy to sell $10,000 as $10—but ONLY if you have all these elements in the place that I'm teaching you.

Your Most Valuable Business Asset

What do you think your most valuable business asset is?

IT'S JUST AS EASY TO SELL $10K AS $10, BUT ONLY IF YOU HAVE ALL THIS IN PLACE.

- Your brain?

- Your mindset?

- Your habits?

- Having more information?

While all of these are important, the answer is *a list of people who know, like and trust you.*

That's because when you have a list of people who know, like and trust you, you can offer your products and services to them far more affordably than advertising to people who don't know, like or trust you.

How to Double Your Online Sales Without Spending a Dime on Ads

If you do this on your own, here's what you'll need to do:

Step 1: Identify the world's top copywriters.

Go to Google type in "world's best copywriters" and you'll get 33.5 million results. Of course, you get a lot of ads (all the top results are ads, you know that by now right?)

So you'll need to sort through the results and compile your list of the world's top copywriters.

Step 2: Build a swipe file of the best email copy from

the world's top copywriters.

A swipe file means you model what they do—you don't copy it, you don't plagiarize. You just take the ideas they have and then you insert your information for your products and services.

Step 3: Organize them so you can "fill in the blanks" based on whatever you need at the moment.

Based on whatever you're selling at that particular time.

Step 4: Deploy these messages so you can build trust and make more sales without spending more on paid advertising.

This means you first do your research, then build your swipe file, then assemble it, then fill in the blanks with your information and send it to your list of contacts so you can sell your products and services.

Remember, you're not plagiarizing, you're not copying. You're modeling what works and then deploy it for your situation.

Ironically, most people think email marketing is writing and sending emails. However, here's what email marketing REALLY is:

Strategy, research, copywriting, editing, approvals, list building, list management, email deliverability, engagement, template design, template creation, collaboration, engineering, device testing, translation, localization, landing page data, data analysis, and a heck of a lot more!

And of course, you have so much free time, right? Basically with nothing to do most days, I'm guessing. (You're picking up on the joke here, right?)

No, you DON'T have enough free time to do all this. You're already too busy with too much to do and not enough time to do it.

So here's another crazy idea: ***You just can get this all done FOR you.***

How would you like to get all of that done FOR you, so you don't have to waste hours or weeks or months or years trying to figure this out like I had to.

I've Done All The Heavy Lifting For You

You're welcome (again)!

In fact, I've assembled all of this just for you. I've created fill in the blank templates that you can right now deploy and start making money from TODAY. Like right now.

Did you know that just this one piece alone cost me over $150,000.00, and an ungodly number of years of my life that I can never get back?

What This Means For You

Imagine it's 12 months from now, and you've gotten all of this heavy lifting done for you. You've got all of the done-for-you templates, checklists, resources and strategies that I've spent over 20 years of my life and more than $750,000 of my own time and money to put together for you.

And you're just laying on the beach and enjoying it, because you just applied it and now it's in place, running on autopilot without you having to lift a finger.

Now imagine you're laying on the beach with your family and friends. You're on vacation and suddenly, your phone dings. You look at your phone and you're like, "Oh look, I just got another online order and had more money drop into my bank account." And you go back to sipping your drink with an umbrella in it.

And your family and friends look at you and say, "Now wait a minute. Just hold on a second. Did you just say you just made more money? You just got money in your bank account just right now? But you're not even doing anything. And money is just landing in your bank account?

THIS CAN BE YOUR NEW REALITY 12 MONTHS FROM NOW.

How the heck did you DO that? Remember last year when we never even saw you, because you were working like a dog. We never saw you at all, and you still weren't making money. What the heck did you DO?"

And you smile and say, "I had a breakthrough!"

Now as you're reading this, some more head trash may

have come up. So let's address that right here and now...

HEAD TRASH: "I'm not sure I can handle the discomfort that may come with this program."

Here's what my client Elizabeth P. has to say...

When I first heard about Noah, I was just starting my business and was confronted with tons of head trash. However, as a result of what I learned from Noah, in less than two years, I had my first seven-figure year. **Today, I'm doing multiple seven figures per year while spending more time with my family. Thank you Noah!**

HEAD TRASH: "I don't know if this is the best use of my time and money."

Here's what my client Mike C. has to say...

Before coaching with Noah, I'd spent over $70,000 on shelf-help and got nowhere. After hiring Noah as my coach, I doubled my income in the first six weeks, then doubled it AGAIN the next six weeks. **That means I doubled my income TWICE in just 12 weeks. Talk about a 12-Week Breakthrough!**

HEAD TRASH: "I don't think I have the energy or resources to do this."

Here's what my client Prem P. has to say...

I came from Thailand with 80% in my pocket

and a young son to take care of. Before coaching with Noah, I was making $4000 a month in my business. ***In the first 12 weeks my income went up $10,000 per month and it just keeps growing!*** Noah helped me so much and he's so humble, he listened to me and told me to speak from my heart. I feel honored to be his student, because he built up my confidence and I'm a new person as a result of learning from him.

Talk about someone who had every excuse NOT to do it! Yet she didn't let her head trash stop her. She took action, followed the formula, and got results.

If they did it, why not me?

This Is All You Need to Succeed

Remember, all you need is the right PLAN, the right TOOLS and the right SUPPORT—however, you also need to take the right ACTION. Because I'll give you the first three elements— but only you can provide the action to make it work, just like the people whose stories I'm sharing with you, and thousands more just like you.

Now let's go to the final piece of the puzzle to become a highly paid, highly sought-after 7-Figure Expert...

CHAPTER 6

Phase Five: 7-Figure Traffic

"When you have a dream you can't let go of, trust your instincts and go for it with all you've got!"
—Harvey Mackay

Now let's examine the final cause of Income Ceiling Syndrome. Remember, the great news for YOU is that if you get any ONE of these problems fixed, you can experience **hockey stick growth** in your business!

Most entrepreneurs are busy being distracted by the latest marketing fad or gimmick. You can't go on social media or even open your email without some marketing guru telling you that if you don't do "this" you're screwed, and this "magic bullet" will fix all your problems.

However, the real issue here is what I call **Invisibility Disorder.** What does that mean and how much is it costing you right now?

Common Symptoms of Invisibility Disorder

- Low conversion rates

- Few or no online sales or leads coming in

- Low email open rates

- Low click-through rates

- Low social media engagement

- Low search engine rankings

- Low visibility on online platforms

- Poor online reputation or no reputation at all

- You're struggling to achieve sustainable growth in the online space

Can you relate to any of these?

Here's What Won't Fix The Problem

While most people aren't even aware of the problem, let alone how to fix it, here's what WON'T fix this problem:

- Ignoring Search Engine Optimization (SEO)

- Neglecting your social media marketing.

- Not creating valuable or shareable content.

- Not building an email list

- Not collaborating with other influencers.

- Getting caught up in analysis paralysis.

- Thinking the problem will magically fix itself.

- Watching Netflix and hoping the problem will go away.

- Working harder and longer without a proven, paint-by-numbers, fill-in-the-blanks SOLUTION

How many of these have you tried or are you currently doing right now?

How Much Is This Costing You?

This is another very important question: ***How much will it cost you in the next 12 months if you don't cure your Invisibility Disorder?***

Now, let me ask you this: ***Would you rather get this problem fixed sooner or later?*** I hope your answer is sooner, rather than later.

Remember, the education system wants to keep you stuck, because it's easier to control a population that doesn't question the status quo. Don't let them keep you stuck any longer, because *the longer you stall, the tougher the haul.*

Phase Five: 7-Figure Traffic

Because this problem is so common and costing you so much money, Phase Five of my 7-Figure Expert Formula is **7-Figure Traffic.** Once you get this in place working for you, you'll start to attract your Ideal Buyers to your Automated Sales Funnels like bees to honey, which means more people will start buying your Irresistible Offers while you sleep (or do whatever you want!).

Three Common Myths About Making Money Online

Myth #1: "The money is in the list."

You've heard this before, right? Every marketing guru out there preaches this morning and night. And they're half right. Here's the TRUTH:

FACT: Your online success in primarily determined by *the quality of the relationship that you have with the people on your list.*

For example, I started my company in 1997—and believe it or not, I still have people on my list who have been with me since the 90s! Because people buy at different speeds: there are fast buyers, medium buyers and slow buyers.

For instance, my client Charles who I told you about earlier read half of one of my books and made an appointment on BreakthroughwithNoah.com. We had one conversation and he paid me $100,000.00 to coach him one-on-one. That's an example of a fast buyer.

These are people who say, "Noah, I've got this problem and I want it fixed NOW. I'm tired of being held back by my head trash. So let's get this fixed!"

Boom—hockey stick growth in record time.

Medium buyers need a little more nurturing. they normally go to my YouTube channel WatchNoahTV.com and watch some of my videos. They'll research and compare, and then they'll buy from me.

Then you have the slow buyers. They might be on your

list for 3 years or more before they buy something. Nothing wrong with that.

The point is, when you treat people on your list as *real people* with real problems, questions, concerns, worries, dreams, hopes and desires, **you can write your own ticket to financial freedom.**

Myth #2: "Social media is all you need."

Lots of gurus are teaching this, too. You see them every time you scroll on social media. Yet here's the TRUTH:

FACT: I've never seen anyone make big money online and achieve financial freedom **unless you own your own online properties.**

Think about it this way: Do you own Facebook or YouTube or Instagram? Unless your name in Mark Zuckerberg or Sergei Brin, the answer is no. That means, the people who do own those social media platforms can do whatever they want—and that includes removing you whenever they feel like it, and there's nothing you can do about it.

Let me tell you a story to illustrate this point. I told you earlier that I grew up poor in a rich neighborhood. What I didn't tell you is that when I was just 15 years old, the bank foreclosed on our home and we were forced out of the home that I grew up in.

My parents had to find a home for us, and since they couldn't afford to buy another home, they had to find a place to rent. There were five of us—my parents and us three kids, my older brother and younger sister.

Amazingly, my parents found a nice house to rent that was in a great location. I was in high school, and this house was about a ten-minute walk to school. So it seemed like everything turned out fine.

One morning, I'm getting ready for school and I come into the kitchen for breakfast, like any other day. However, on this day, I see my mother standing over the kitchen sink and she's crying.

THIS WAS THE DAY LIFE CHANGED FOR MY FAMILY AGAIN.

I say, "Mom, what's wrong?" She says, "The landlord just told us that he's going to sell this house and we've got to move again."

It had only been a few months since we moved into this house, not even a year. And now we had to move again.

It was a nightmare. Since my parents still didn't have any money, they were forced to find another house, and the only one they could find was, to put it kindly, a lousy one.

My parents ended up living there for nearly a decade, even though we all hated that house. It took them another ten years to get back on their feet and finally build a new house, that they still live in to this day.

What's the point of this story and what does it mean for you?

The point is that if don't own your own property, someone can kick you out anytime they want. And since you don't own any of these social media platforms, that means they can kick you off any time they want, with or without a case, and there's nothing you can do about it.

Do you know someone, maybe a friend or colleague, who had built their entire business on a platform, only to see their account wiped out overnight? We've all heard the horror stories, and they're real.

The point is that I don't want to see this happen to YOU.

I want YOU empowered.

I want YOU in control of your own destiny.

Fact is, I own more than 300 unique web properties. That means nobody can kick me out! That means I'm in control of my own destiny. That means I'm in charge.

Now you certainly don't need to own 300 web properties like I do. But I certainly believe that you need to own at least ONE web property (domain) that YOU control and YOU are in charge of—because that's the best way to control your own destiny.

Myth #3: "Making money online is difficult."

If you don't know what you're doing, almost anything is difficult—because you're stumbling around in the dark, trying to figure it out for yourself. However, here's the TRUTH:

FACT: Making money online does NOT require creativity or even willpower. *It's a system, a formula.*

Making money online is like building a house. Most experts and entrepreneurs get up in the morning, and start slapping boards together, hoping a house shows up. But that's not how you build a house.

All you need is the right PLAN, the right TOOLS, and the right SUPPORT. And once you have this in place working for you...

- You'll consistently meet or exceed your financial goals.

- You'll have a clear direction and vision for your business.

- You'll have a strong team and support system in place.

- You'll have a diverse range of income streams.

- You'll have a highly scalable business model.

- You'll have a strong online presence and reputation.

- You'll have a clear defined target audience and customer base.

- You'll have a strong marketing strategy in place.

- You'll have a strong value proposition.

- You'll have a strong network of connections in your industry.

And that means you'll get all of these benefits, too...

- You'll have systems that make money on autopilot.

- You'll stop sacrificing time for dollars.

- You'll stop being a time for money worker.

- You'll have a high level of motivation and drive.

- You'll be able to focus and finish.

- You'll gain more respect and recognition.

- You'll have more success attracting customers and clients.

- You'll have more success generating leads and sales.

- You'll have more impact, more influence and more income.

Imagine being able to walk into a car dealership, picking the one you want, and not worrying about the payments—you can even pay cash if you want!

Imagine taking your family have fun vacations that you talk about and cherish for the rest of your lives.

Or just staying home, enjoying more time with your spouse, your kids, your grandkids, your pets, your hobbies, or just taking more time off.

Dr. Noah's 7-Figure M.A.P.S.S.S. Method to Cure Invisibility Disorder

If you want to cure your Invisibility Disorder, here's my legendary M.A.P.S.S.S. Method to drive targeted traffic to your Automated Sales Funnels:

M stands for MEDIA.

MEDIA are the collective communication outlets used to deliver information. Your main media outlets are:

- TV (local and national)

- Radio (local and national)

- Blogs

- Podcasts

- Newspapers (yes, they still exist)

- Magazines (print and online)

- Your own newsletter (email and/or print)

To see dozens of examples of how to do this, visit my Online Press Room at **https://NoahStJohn.com/media.**

A stands for AFFILIATE MARKETING.

AFFILIATE MARKETING is a type of performance-based marketing in which you reward people for each customer brought to you by the affiliate's own marketing efforts. Here's how it works:

1. People tell their list members about your products.
2. People buy your products using your affiliate's custom links.
3. You pay your affiliates sales commissions for every sale that comes from their affiliate link.

More about affiliate marketing below.

P stands for PAY PER CLICK ADVERTISING.

PAY PER CLICK ADVERTISING is a form of internet marketing in which you pay a fee each time one of your ads is clicked. Here's how it works:

1. Create an ad in one of the major traffic networks (Google, YouTube, Bing, Facebook, Instagram, etc.)

2. You pay the network each time your ad is clicked.

3. Optimize and scale your ads to increase profit over time.

S stands for SPEAKING.

There are four types of SPEAKING that make you money:

1. Speak-to-sell

2. Speak to Collect Leads

3. Corporate consulting

4. Your own live or virtual events

To see examples of how to do this, visit my Speaker page at **https://NoahStJohn.com/book-noah**

S stands for SEO (Search Engine Optimization).

SEO is the process of affecting the visibility of your content in a search engine's unpaid results, often referred to as "organic". Here's how it works:

1. Create blog posts and/or videos about topics related to your target market.

2. Your content gets ranked by the search engines (Google, Bing, etc.)

3. Prospects buy from you as a result of engaging with your free content.

To see examples of how to do this, visit my blog at **https://NoahStJohn.com/blog** and subscribe to my YouTube channel at **https://WatchNoahTV.com.**

S stands for SOCIAL MEDIA MARKETING.

SOCIAL MEDIA MARKETING (SMM) is The use of social media platforms to promote your products or services. Here's how it works:

1. Create a series of social media posts that entice people to engage with your content on the main social media platforms (Facebook, Instagram, LinkedIn, etc.)

2. Encourage people to visit your Automated Sales Funnel to get more valuable content (i.e., your products or services).

3. Prospects buy from you as a result of engaging with your free content.

If You Want Something You've Never Had...

...you've got to do something you've never done. Doesn't that just make sense? Because you know the definition of insanity—doing the same thing and expecting different results.

How would you like to make money from me in the next 45 days without even having to build anything? Here's how to do it—simply become one of my affiliates!

Step 1: Sign up for my FREE affiliate program at **https://NoahStJohn.com/jv**

Simply fill out the form and enter your PayPal information so I can start paying you. There's no cost to you, and it will only take you about 60 seconds.

Step 2: login to Affiliate Dashboard and select the program you'd like to promote.

When you login to your Affiliate Dashboard, you'll see a list of my events and programs that you can promote (see **https://ShopNoahStJohn.com** for a complete list of programs and events), along with your custom affiliate link and swipe copy.

Step 3: Use the swipe copy that I've created for you and share your unique link via email or social media.

After spending hundreds of thousands of dollars on copywriting and marketing programs, I've pre-written all of the high-converting emails and social media posts that you can share with your friends and colleagues.

Step 4: Start earning commissions on every sale!

Yes, I will PAY YOU commissions for every sale that comes when you refer people to my life-changing programs and events that your friends and colleagues will absolutely

love!

Remember, I give you all the fill-in-the-blank, copy and paste templates, which means all you have to do is send a few emails or post on your social media accounts. The fact is, I pay mt affiliates thousands of dollars every month. Why not YOU?

Now as you're reading this, some more head trash may have come up. So let's address that right here and now...

HEAD TRASH: "I already know this stuff."
Here's what my client Matt D. has to say...

> ***"I've seen my client list increase more in just 12 weeks than all of last year*** because of coaching with Noah. Noah St. John is the real deal!"

And Matt owns a marketing agency! So even though he "knew this stuff," there was still quite a bit that he wasn't actually DOING. And once he started implementing, he got hockey stick growth. ***If it worked for him, why not YOU?***

HEAD TRASH: "This sounds too good to be true."
Here's what my client Brandon H. has to say...

> "Before finding Noah, I had spent over $40,000 on all those other sales and self-help programs with no results. ***As a result of coaching with Noah, my sales TRIPLED in just 30 days, and by the end of the year, my sales increased by 560%.*** Thank You Noah for changing my life!"

When Are You Going to Stop Losing Money?

I want you to add up all the money you're losing because you don't have this in place right now. I'll bet you're losing at least $10,000 each and every month because you don't have this working for you right now. In fact, it's probably closer to $50,000 to $100,000 a month, or more.

So I want you to ask yourself, ***when am I going to stop losing out on that money?*** When am I going to stop paying $10,000, $25,000, $50,000 or $100,000 per month that I'm losing right now?

Just imagine how good it's going to feel when you go from your Current Limited Identity that says you "can't" do it, to your New Desired identity that KNOWS you CAN do it.

How much would you invest if you could put $1 in and get back $2 in net profit? In other words, if you invest one dollar and you get back two dollars in net profit, your just doubled your money. So how much would you invest if that were the case?

Right: the correct answer is: EVERYTHING.

So the question now is...

What are you waiting for?

CHAPTER 7
For Those Who Want to Go Further and Faster

*"Lots of people have dreams and get knocked down
and don't have things go their way.
Just keep getting up and getting up,
and then you WILL get your breakthrough!"*
—Tom Brady

Now that this book is almost over, you have three options:

Option 1: Forget everything you just read and let this become more "shelf-help."

Option 2: Try to figure all this out on your own.

Option 3: Do it with me so we can ACCELERATE your results up to 10 times faster with less stress and no time wasted.

So if you want to...

- Take out your head trash without using affirmations, vision boards or chanting mantras for hours on end

- Get your foot off the brake without having to use willpower or motivation

- Cure your Inferior Offer Disorder so you have Irresistible Offers that have your Ideal Buyers begging to give you money

- Replace your Franken-Funnels with Automated Sales Funnels that make you money while you sleep

- Overcome Invisibility Disorder so you have more impact, influence and income without spending a dime on paid ads

...you're invited to join ***The 12-Week Breakthrough.***

Because in just 12 short weeks, I'll give you my copy and paste, plug-and-play, paint-by-numbers, fill-in-the-blank templates, checklists, resources and strategies that have generated over $31 million in online sales and more than $2.8 BILLION in found revenues for me and my clients since 1997.

If All This Did was...

If all this did was finally help you **shatter** the Income Ceiling that's been limiting your potential, without the pain and expense of trying to figure it out on your own, *wouldn't that be worth it?*

If all this did was give you the power to **transform** your deepest fears into your biggest motivators, so you can finally have more impact, influence and income without the overwhelm, *wouldn't that be worth it?*

In fact, if all this did was equip you to cultivate the habits that separate the **extraordinarily successful** from everyone else, so you can make more money while winning your life back, *wouldn't that be worth it?*

Remember, I had to spend over $750,000 and over 20 years of my life (that I can't get back) to figure all this out, running around to all these marketing gurus who can't teach their way out of a paper bag.

Here's What this Means For You

1. You don't have to go through the pain, torment and agony that I did to figure all this out on my own.

2. You have hidden equity in your business right now. However...

3. The longer you wait to get all of this in place working for you, the more money, opportunity and wealth will slip through your fingers.

Because the more you delay, the more you'll pay.

Picture Your Life 12 Weeks From Today

Walk with me for a moment, 12 weeks from today. Imagine that we start working together right now. Did you notice how much **happier** you are right now?

How you're **sleeping** better and more peacefully?

How you start the day with a sense of **joy and purpose**?

How life feels **fresh, full of potential, less constrained**?

All as a result of you taking action right now.

...

Now picture your life 12 weeks from today if you DON'T take action.

Notice how everything's the same.

Exactly the same as it is now.

Notice how you still have the same problems, the same frustrations, the same unanswered questions, the same stress, the same confusion, the same overwhelm, the same endless searching for a solution that was right in front of your face.

All because you didn't take action on what was right in front of you.

The choice is yours.

...

Now as you're reading this, some more head trash may have come up. So let's address that right here and now...

HEAD TRASH: "I'm not sure if this is a good fit for me."
Here's what my client Adam S. has to say...

"I'm here to tell you that Noah St. John's coaching is fantastic! **Since we started working with Noah, my company grew six times in size.** When you work with Noah, he focuses on removing all the things that are holding you back, whereas a lot of other people out there are all focused on pushing you forward, not realizing that when your foot is on the brake at the same time that it's on the gas pedal, you're just getting in your own way. So my recommendation, my GUARANTEE is: give coaching with Noah a shot, you're going to be 100% happy with it"

HEAD TRASH: "I don't think I can afford it."

Here's what my client Thomesa L. has to say...

"Before Noah, I was a seminar junkie. Yes, I went through program after program just doing what I could to better myself personally and professionally. When I discovered Noah St. John, I had that fear of, 'Is this just another program that I may get a few nuggets from and then just go back to my default program?'

Well, my fear is gone! I bit the bullet, I jumped into Noahs program and i couldn't be happier, because he is DIFFERENT. He is really practical in talking about what is unconscious in your being so that you can bring it to the forefront of your consciousness and make a real change. When he talks about Power Habits, they are POWERFUL habits for your life and your well-being. **In the first two weeks, I TRIPLED my investment!**

Does that make you a little more excited about where you are going with Noah? So I just want to say that if you are on the fence about any program that Noah is offering. GET OFF! Take action. It works. It's simple, it's practical. And you'll be amazed at what you gain from it.

Now, I think Noah's coaching is for everyone. but it's definitely for you if you're skeptical, if you've been 'seminar junkied' to death, or have hit a plateau in your business or personal life. So get in NOW, because I'm here to tell you I am absolutely thrilled that I took that leap of faith. Thank you, Noah for all you have taught me!"

HEAD TRASH: "What if I don't get a return on my investment?

Here's what my client Clendra M. has to say...

"Noah's coaching created MOMENTUM in ALL areas of my life—business, health, love and more. **I made my investment back in less than 48 hours after joining!** The modules, the bonuses, the access to a community of people around the world—it's all been priceless!"

This Isn't For Everyone

Now I have to be crystal clear: This program is NOT for everyone. For example...

- This is NOT for people looking for "get rich quick."

- This is NOT for those who want to stay stuck in confusion, victimhood.

- This is NOT for people who want to do everything themselves.

- This is NOT for those who are waiting for everything to be perfect before taking action (because nothing's ever "perfect")

However, this IS right for you if...

✓ You're standing on the **brink of greatness**, yet you need the final push to step over your internal hurdles and achieve the success you deserve.

✓ You're feeling the pressure of your **untapped potential.**

✓ You're ready to **unleash your true power** and reshape your life.

✓ You want to **silence the nagging voice of doubt** and replace it with self-confidence and assertiveness.

✓ You're seeking to **escape the trap of endless 'busyness'** and instead, craft a life of impactful productivity.

✓ You're committed to making this **your best year yet**—not just in terms of wealth, but happiness, health and relationships, too.

✓ You're ready to end the struggle, **stop fighting against yourself**, and start aligning with the current of success that flows within YOU.

Here's What to Do Now

If you're a Fast Buyer and you know you want this and you want it NOW, go to

https://12WeekBreakthrough.com/money-maker

For instance, if you're ready right now (like my client Charles who gave me a dollar and I gave him eighteen dollars back), that's where you can secure your spot with a small deposit and then someone from my team will contact you to make sure you're a good fit for the program. Plus, when you submit your deposit, you'll also be eligible for a Bonus VIP Coaching Session with me! If you're a Medium Speed Buyer and you want to talk with someone first, then go to **https:// BreakthroughwithNoah.com** watch the 11-minute video and submit your application. (Note: Medium Buyers are not eligible to get the Bonus VIP Coaching Session with me.)

What Happens Next

After you secure your deposit or submit your application, my team and I will evaluate your application, and if we think there's a fit, someone from my team will contact you by email. If we think it's not a fit, we'll tell you that too.

Either way, you're going to receive our legendary white glove VIP service that we are famous for.

The fact is, I've seen millions made from even taking the wrong actions, but I've never seen anything good came from not taking action.

...Remember, I'm going to give you...

- **The Right PLAN** (show you what to do)

- **The Right TOOLS** (show you how to do it)

- **The Right SUPPORT** (believe in you, even if you don't believe in yourself yet)

However, I can't make you take *The Right Actions*. Only YOU can do that. Remember, if you don't have these things in place, here's what's going to happen...

- If you don't have the right PLAN, you'll stay STUCK.

- If you don't have the right TOOLS, you'll be OVERWHELMED.

- If you don't have the right SUPPORT, you'll feel ALONE.

- And if you don't take the right ACTION, what will happen is...**NOTHING.**

How Your Life Can Change In Just 12 Weeks

As we come to the conclusion of this book, let me tell you a true story about how your life can change in just 12 short weeks.

In November 2020, the world was in the depths of the global pandemic. It seemed like everything was shut down and nobody was doing anything. It was all fear, fear, fear.

On the Saturday before Thanksgiving 2020, I woke up at six in the morning with a vision. Now this totally came out of the blue, but I had a vision that said, *"We're supposed to move."*

Have you ever had one of those visions or inner knowings that just said something totally off the wall? Something that didn't make any logical sense—yet you listened to it, because you know it came from your higher knowing or intuitive self, the part of you that's beyond the rational and beyond the logical. You've had that happen to you too, right?

So when this happened to me, I'm like, *What?*

Because my wife and I were living in a nice, upper middle-class home. Moving to a new house was the furthest thing from my mind.

Yet I couldn't shake this inner knowing, this vision that woke me up early that morning. So I thought, maybe we can move in, say, six months to a year. *After all, there's no hurry, right?*

So I get up, turn on my computer, and start looking on real estate websites for homes in my area. Click, click, click. With no sense of urgency or even what I was looking for.

Suddenly, I came upon this house, this mansion on a hill, and I looked at it like: *WHAT?*

This house is *stunning.*

This house is *incredible.*

This house is a *mansion on a hill.*

And it's *in my price range.*

And it's only *10 minutes from where I'm sitting right now.*

And *the price just dropped.*

And *there was going to be an open house the next day—* yes, the Sunday before Thanksgiving 2020.

So I wake up Babette and say, "Honey, you wanna go look at a house tomorrow?"

She says, "Sure!"

The next day, as we pull up the driveway to this mansion on a hill, she takes one look at the house, looks at me and says, "I'm packing tonight."

83 days later, we moved into that mansion on a hill.

Friend, that's just one day less than 12 weeks. And we celebrated our 10th wedding anniversary in our new mansion on a hill.

So yes, your life CAN change in less than 12 weeks—if you're willing to take the ACTION to make it happen!

...

Napoleon Hill said, "Those who reach decisions promptly and definitely know what they want and generally get it. The leaders in every walk of life decide quickly and firmly."

W. Clement Stone said, "The greatest enemy of wealth isn't a mindset issue. It isn't wealth or resources, it isn't even upbringing or circumstances. The greatest enemy of wealth is DELAY."

Dr. Noah St. John says, ***"Procrastination is the assassination of your destination."***

Our Final Guarantee

Ben Franklin said many years ago that there are only two guarantees in life: death and taxes. With all due respect to ol' Ben, I would argue there is, in fact, a third guarantee. And that is this:

If you keep doing the same thing you're doing now, I guarantee you'll keep getting the same results you're getting now.

Therefore, if you'd like to get BETTER results in your life and your business, I encourage you take ACTION now—because time waits for no one!

"Noah St. John's coaching starts where Think and Grow Rich and The Secret left off!"
—Mike Filsaime, 8-Figure CEO of Groove.cm

"My company went from being stuck at $4M in sales to over $20M in sales as a result of coaching with Noah!
—Adam S., Eight-Figure CEO

"My income is up 800% since I started coaching with Noah!"
—Steven B., Entrepreneur

"Coaching with Noah enabled me to double my business in less that twelve months after I've been stuck at the same level for fifteen years!"
—Aubrey R., Entrepreneur

"In the first two weeks of coaching with Noah, I TRIPLED my investment!"
—Thomesa L., Entrepreneur

"As a result of coaching with Noah, I doubled my income, then doubled it AGAIN in Just 12 short weeks!"
—Mike C., Entrepreneur

CHAPTER 8
RECOMMENDED RESOURCES

YOUR FREE BONUS GIFT

As a thank-you for purchasing this book, I would like to give you exclusive, insider access to the exact system my clients are using to instantly shatter their limiting beliefs that were putting a ceiling on their business revenue, once and for all, using ONE simple process that can take as little as five minutes a day.

Best of all, it works especially well even when all the other programs, seminars, methods, systems and gurus have let you down or you don't actually know what the specific problem is.

This is also the fastest and easiest way to gain special access to the lucrative system that's added more than $2.8 billion in revenue for me and my clients since 1997.

So if you...

- Want a proven system to instantly shatter limiting beliefs and recapture lost revenues

- Have a business that's beyond start-up phase and is actually making sales

- Are ready for "hockey stick growth" in your company

- Want insider access to my fill-in-the-blank templates, checklists and resources

- Want to know how this guaranteed system can work for you

Schedule your complimentary 7-Figure Breakthrough Session now, because we will review your business, see how this system can work for you, offer you some advice on how to use it, and then discuss (if we know we can help you) how we can help you implement it—GUARANTEED.

Book your Breakthrough Consultation at **BreakthroughwithNoah.com**

Book Noah to Speak

"Noah is definitely NOT your typical motivational speaker! I took six pages of notes during his keynote presentation. SIMPLY PHENOMENAL- A-MUST HAVE RESOURCE for every organization that wants to grow!"
— Mary Kay Cosmetics

"All I heard was great feedback! Thank you, Noah, for really engaging our audience I am recommending you as a speaker for more meetings."
— Meeting Planners International

"I highly recommend Noah St. John as a keynote speaker because he resonates on a deep emotional level with his audience. Dynamic, impactful, inspiring, motivating, and professional- in short, the PERFECT speaker!"
— City Summit & Gala

Book Noah as your keynote speaker, and you're guaranteed to make your event highly enjoyable and unforgettable.

For more than two decades, Noah St. John has consistently rated as the #1 keynote speaker by meeting planners and attendees.

His unique style combines inspiring audiences with his remarkable TRUE story, keeping them laughing with his high-energy, down-to-earth style, and empowering them with actionable strategies to take their RESULTS to the NEXT LEVEL.

Book Noah for your event at
BookNoah.com

Also Available from Dr. Noah St. John

BREAKTHROUGH WITH NOAH

Discover How My Clients Are Instantly Shattering Their
Limiting Beliefs That Were Putting A Ceiling On Their
Revenue, Once And For All, Using 1 Simple Process That
Can Take Place In As Little As 5 Minutes a Day.
BreakthroughwithNoah.com

POWER HABITS® ACADEMY

Take Out Your Head Trash About Money, Admit What You
Truly Desire and Experience Your Quantum Leap.
PowerHabitsAcademy.com

THE AFFORMATIONS® ADVANTAGE

Immediately Attract More Abundance on Autopilot.
Afformations.com

Shop our complete line of business and
personal growth programs:
ShopNoahStJohn.com

Book Noah to speak at your virtual or live event:
BookNoah.com

Motivate and Inspire Others!

"SHARE THIS BOOK"

RETAIL $19.95

Special Quantity Discounts Available

To Place an Order, Contact:

(330) 871-4331

support@SuccessClinic.com

Acknowledgements

My Most Grateful Thanks to . . .

God, the answer to all of our questions.

My beautiful wife, Babette, for being my best friend and the best Loving Mirror I've ever had. Thank you for believing in me and supporting me and for your tireless commitment to helping me put a dent in the universe.

My parents, who sacrificed and gave more than they had.

Jack Canfield, for grokking my message when it was a bunch of pages bound with a piece of tape.

Dr. Stephen W. Covey, who inspired me to get into the business of helping people when the audio cassette album of *The 7 Habits of Highly Effective People* fell of a church bookshelf and landed at my feet. I swear I'm not making that up.

Through the years, many have shared ideas, inspiration, mentoring, and support that have impacted my life, each in a different way. While it's impossible to thank everyone, please know that I appreciate you greatly:

Alex Mandossian, Arianna Huffington, Donny Osmond, Gary Vaynerchuk, Jenny McCarthy, Joel Osteen, John Lee Dumas, Marie Forleo, Suze Orman, Anik Singal, Ashley Grayson, Dan Bova, David Meltzer, Doug Crowe, Dr. Fabrizio Mancini, Harvey Mackay, Jason Hewlett, Jay Abraham, Jeff Lerner, Jeff Magee, Jen Groover, Joe Vitale, John Assaraf, John Cito, Dr. John Gray, Jon Benson, Mike Filsaime, Nathan

Osmond, Neale Donald Walsch, Peter Hoppenfeld, Rich Schefren, Richard Rossi, Russell Brunson, Tom Junod, Verne Harnish, and so many other people who have inspired me in my career!

Very special thanks to the vast and growing tribe of our phenomenal coaching clients around the world who believe in the power of this message. Thank you for spreading the word about my work to all corners of the globe!

Every day, as I hear more and more stories of how the coaching work we do together is changing lives, you inspire, encourage, and uplift me.

I am humbled by your stories of how my work has changed your lives—truly, more than you know. Whether you're a member of our Coaching Family, attend one of our virtual events or online trainings this year, or simply commit to telling your friends about this book, I'm grateful for you.

Every day brings with it the opportunity to be reborn in the next greatest version of ourselves.

NOW IT'S YOUR TURN
I LOOK FORWARD TO BEING A PART OF YOUR SUCCESS STORY!

About The Author

NOAH ST. JOHN, PhD is recognized as "The Father of AFFORMATIONS®" and "The Mental Health Coach to the Stars."

Working with Hollywood celebrities, seven- and eight-figure company CEOs, professional athletes, top executives, and elite entrepreneurs, Noah is famous for helping his coaching clients make more in twelve weeks than they did in the previous twelve months while gaining 1-3 hours per day and 4-8 weeks a year.

Noah's clients are the 0.1% rock stars who love to *take action* and get amazing *results*!

Noah is also the only author in history to have works Published by HarperCollins, Hay House, Simon & Schuster, Mind valley, Nightingale-Conant, and the *Chicken Soup for the Soul* publisher. His eighteen books have been published in nineteen languages worldwide.

Noah's mission is to eliminate not-enoughness from the world, and he is internationally known for his signature coaching services and facilitating workshops at companies and institutions across the globe. Noah delivers private workshops, virtual events, and online courses that his audiences call "MANDATORY" for anyone who wants to succeed in life and business."

One of the most requested, in-demand business and motivational keynote speakers in the world, Noah is famous for having "The Midas Torch" became his clients have added more than $2.8 billion in found revenues. His sought-after advice is known as the "secret sauce" to business and personal growth.

He also appears frequently in the news worldwide, including ABC, NBC, CBS, FOX, The Hallmark Channel, National Public Radio, *Chicago Sun-Times, Parade, Los Angeles Business Journal, The Washington Post, Woman's Day, Entrepreneurs on Fire, Selling Power,* Entrepreneur. com, *The Jenny McCarthy Show, Costco Connection,* and *SUCCESS* magazine.

Fun fact: Noah once won an all-expenses-paid trip to Hawaii on the game show Concentration, where he missed winning a new car by three seconds. (Note: He had not yet discovered his Afformations® Method or Power Habits® Formula.)

Book Noah to speak for your next virtual or live event, conference, or seminar at **BookNoah.com.**

Made in United States
Troutdale, OR
08/05/2024

21769434R00083